Gallery Books
Editor: Peter Fallon

HIS SKALDCRANE'S NEST

By the same author

His Skaldcrane's Nest, poems, The Gallery Press, Dublin, 1979
The Headgear of the Tribe, new and selected poems, edited by Peter Fallon, The Gallery Press, 1979
A Limerick Rake, versions from the Irish, The Gallery Press, 1978
The Gododdin, translations (with illustrations by Louis le Brocquy), The Dolmen Press, Dublin, 1977
Sing Me Creation, poems, The Gallery Press, 1977
Stations, poems (with illustrations by Margo Veillon), American University in Cairo Press, 1976
Separations, poems, The Goldsmith Press, Dublin, 1973
Hellas, poems, New Writers' Press, Dublin, 1971
The Dying Gaul, poems, MacGibbon and Kee, London, 1968
Off Licence, translations, The Dolmen Press, 1968
The Dark Edge of Europe, poems, MacGibbon and Kee, 1967
Separazioni, poems (with Italian translations), Edizioni Europei, Rome, 1965
Professor Kelleher and the Charles River, a poem, Carthage Press, Cambridge, Mass., 1964
Reilly, poems, The Phoenix Press, London, 1961
Chords and Orchestrations, poems, The Echo Press, Limerick, 1956

Desmond O'Grady

His Skaldcrane's Nest

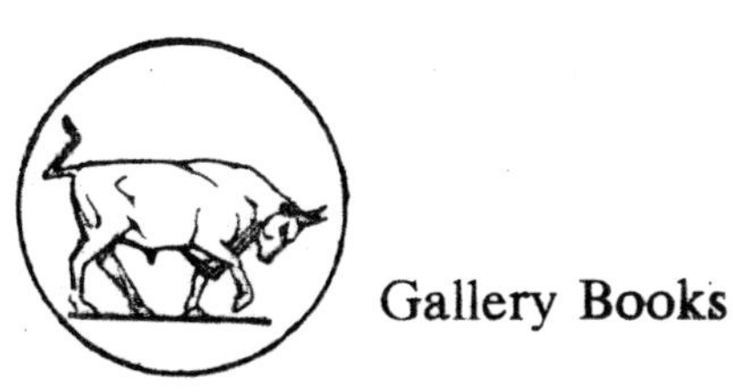

Gallery Books

His Skaldcrane's Nest
is published simultaneously
in paperback and in a
clothbound edition.

The Gallery Press
19 Oakdown Road
Dublin 14
Ireland.

© Desmond O'Grady 1979

Acknowledgements
   Acknowledgements are due to the editors of *The Castle Poets 1977*, *New Irish Writing* (The Irish Press), *The Limerick Socialist*, *Stations* (American University Press, Cairo), and *The Stony Thursday Book* where some of these poems were first published.
   The Gallery Press gratefully acknowledges the assistance of An Chomhairle Ealaíon (The Arts Council of Ireland) towards the publication of this book.

Contents

for Thomas and Moira O'Grady

Pendulum

Easter

Our greentree Easter's round again,
proclaims resurrection. Here in my farm-
house of hospitable bread I pietà
her Greek Calabrian maiden motherhood.
The corn's golden. The grape gangs blood
from the Ides of March in the groin.

Friends. Family. The women bring
this land's various flowers and grain.
Upon my table two small reproductions:
one an Egyptian mummy's sarcophagus;
the other a Cycladic figurine flautist.
His thrown back head sounds out his music.
With ecstacy or vision his musician's eyes
are closed or blind. Ground in the mill
that's winter, I've nothing done; work
in the wood of deep ancestral darkness
knowing flame light wakes all, but not
the scorching flame. So be it so.

The shapes beyond my window
suggest the shapes to come, composed
of sphere, cylinder, square and cone.
Begin again with cone and square,
leave winter with last year. Describe
what's palpable — straight, unadorned, clear;
order, form on the sensuous; to make
a thing of balance, serenity, devoid
destruction, that gives delight and hurts not.

Crisis '74

for Ingrid

This whips all years for crises.
Family, old friends — our parents'
generation — dying now. We're that age.
Emperors, Monarchs, Presidents disgraced, out.
Arab Catholic Protestant Jew
wage dicey war and peace.
Everywhere bristles breakup . . .

Here in Greece
the hawks have blundered Cyprus.
Turkey's moved. The Tyrants topple.
Our island boys, mobilized,
bundle their few belongings into baskets,
battered cases, fourcornered kerchiefs, hustle
on the hectic harbour, await forced transport
to the mainland and military stations.
Women and children break, weep openly in kitchens,
chapels, the common marketplace. Ancestral war.
We, foreigners here, grieve their grief.

Strangers to them and to each other,
met on this summer island, we
fail to ease ourselves much personal crisis
lugged like luggage with us. Daily
we walk the shore — you, me,
your two children — talk. I too
have a boy and girl miles from us here,
to me familiar, where all I pass speaks
ten years' faith and failure. My son's
your boy's age; my daughter a young woman.

In crisis I retreat, choose silence,
mouth monosyllables at straight questions
as an accused man might — but know you,
I'm with you in my silence where only our
affection speaks. Like you, I fear all new
involvement, can only come part way from need,
in dread. But should you come the more
I'm speechless yours at any hour.

We walk, talk shy trivia, at times confront
our own human hiatus: blind dreams, marriage,
children, breakup's chaos. We're confused
as children who soil their pants in public first time.
I take you in — glanced sideways: long-legged,
noble-headed, dark-fleshed. Characteristics
of my loved son's mother, gone absent.
You could have mothered mine
as much your own.

Your son and I swim out with masks
and dive; we loot the seafloor's fleamarket
of small treasures for you. You
wait ashore. I'm your boy's temporary
father. It's our caveman male way
to do you honour, show affection. He
wants to play the man, I the boy.

In bed before lights out, he says he'll work
the fishingboats to help you make a new home here.
Pause. Then he asks you straight if I'd be nice
as now, always. My own son must,
by now, have said the same some other where.
We big-fish adults, flounder and gulp air.
We know it's actions, not fast words, that count.
We say so every time, promise, then disappoint.

Naoussa

Her Summer Visit

for Florence Tamburro

1
And the long wait was not in vain
after all. After the distant places
and the arrogance of frightened people;
after that wandering, a madman, those empty
rooms talking to our pictures, bookshelves,
left faded geegaws of erased summers; after
dark nights on islands with oil lamps
and tears for the stars; after our anguish
of self preservation, our tears on the crowded
thoroughfares of labour, our losing the one
from the other, our nakedness, emptiness,
rejection and claw for what's stable.
Not in vain the long wait nor in vain
our longing in the wastes of endless snows,
endless deserts under a pitiless sky.
There was a homecoming and a gathering
into arms and long hair let down on the pillow;
there was the murmur of tired voices at night
and the shadows of the meanwhile dead in their
corners and the resting with clasped fingers
under the bamboo and seaweed ceiling and the moon.

2
The sun's stuck strongly up outside.
That first boat's passed to pull last night's
dropped nets. You sleep, spreadeagled,
fast in our seaside country bed beneath
our bamboo ceiling — wild flowers from Mount
Vigla altared round you. Our children shrine
far off this morning. We're alone again.
My donkey bawls outside. I go draw water
from the well. Beyond, the sea's
an album of childhood memories . . . My Lady
sleep the sleep of the arrived returner,
dread the dreams of devastated lovers.
Ours wreaked anger not unasked for, our
anguish without answer, I admit now.
Your presence prints that of the moon
on this our sea this night. Your eyes

my blackbacked notebooks filled, lost;
death of relatives, friends. Your carved lips'
labial cadences won't scribe my page . . . Rest
all your southern strength now. We'll need it
for whisper, ache and memory this midnight. Yours . . .

3
Those two seabirds have flown.
Every night, calling each other,
they fly into our sea dingle.
Last night you returned home, slept.
We lay, two calling seabirds
all night darkling and you're still
asleep in our sea single morning.

4
The boy passed my window
with his water bucket, came back
on his donkey. The donkey drank
while the boy tied his hobble rope.
Then he saddled her with the wooden
saddle brace, placed the bucket back
by the well wall, mounted sideways
and, pumping his heels, trotted away.
You slept through all this early
morning activity conducted in silence
like a religious ceremony commemorating
your welcome advent.

5
You comb out your long dark hair
this summer morning in the cool
of our bedroom. The night's hot
sheets thrown over the iron rail
of our house's bed for airing.
You're off to the village for supplies.
I sit to my work table with organ music.

We begin this new day in peace. After much
hardship of spirit we have found reconciliation
of the odds against us. Your suntanned face,
your noble head held stately as a caryatid,
you stride down the rocks below my window
in flowing gallobean white, hair flying behind.

St. Dimitrios' Day

for Nora Ludin

One raw moment between us . . .
Morning. Wake with the sun's
rise over my island's vertebrae. Stalk
into the mother of pearl sea, shell-smooth
since the north wind dropped. You swim
out far — your last this year. I only
enough to get over the genital shock
of early morning's seawater. No one's
about. Back for breakfast: fruit, coffee.
I muse how you always eat apples after love
like an oriental. Today you leave for
your North. I wear your black neckerchief.

While you squirrel your things into your sack
I sit at this table, the door between us open —
that contact need of presence — and scribble.
Then, time to go. I call your name. No
reply. Call again. Silence, except for
the lips' whisper of the silver sea. I'm
suddenly cold. Check every room. Empty.
You've gone. I rush out on the terrace.
I sight you suddenly, far off along
the shore, started for the village.
Muddled, I shout your name. A gull
veers off my voice's vibrations. You
stop, turn, wait. Waving like a warrior
I career to you at reinless gallop. Face
to face. Angry, I talk at you — loud,
rough — then stride on ahead . . .

You catch me up. The sun blazes.
We both burn. You cut: "Don't
ever shout at me again like that."
Pause. Blood pulsates. Eyes forward:
"Why did you run away? I wanted us
to leave that house together."
Your head turns. You're wounded.
"You walked away from me just now."
Still hurt, proud, I swipe: "I've
never walked away from anything. Never!"

14

We walk the lace fringed edge of the steel
faced sea as we've daily done these weeks.
No talk. Finally, backing down, but
with bravura: "Sorry I shouted at you."
Pause. Head down, you whisper to the sand,
like the waves to the wind: "I wanted
to shorten the pain of leaving." Pause. Then,
the woman you: "Shout at me any time you like".
We stop. Tableau. We laugh. Clasp
hands. Clasp heads. Tousle hair.
Walk on — our last barrier dropped
like clothes. We're now each other's.

Morning in the village harbour: deck
wash, net stacks, small cups
of turko-black coffee, boxed
fresh fish, boat business.
In Strati's café they celebrate
St. Dimitros' Day with whiskey off
a foreign vessel and fish grilled
over charcoal on a terracotta pot.
Today's the day we taste the new wine.
It turns into your farewell party —
jokes, laughter, toasts. You're sad.
I sport your black silk neckerchief.
Then time again to go: "Goodbye. Adio.
Farewell. Safe journey. Next year.
Goodbye. Next year." Antiphony.
At your ship I settle your bags
on board. Blind embrace. Farewells.

The moon rose ringed tonight.
Aphrodite its pilot. This light, these
islands, this bay — a Japanese print.
Dark against deep lapis lazuli skies,
Mount Vigla's my Mount Taishan.
The village lights go on across the bay —
candles on a white altar. In Strati's café,
across our winkle whorled cove, they're still
singing and drinking St. Dimitrios.
Not there, we two now mark the three
points of our geographical triangle —
time, space, thought.

The southwest wind
blows up behind
my house. Waves
beyond my window —
tops tipped silver
as your hair caught
by the late summer's sun.
Here comes the storm
will wash away
our hidden harm
this St. Dimitrios' Day.

Midvoyage

for Patricia Mitchell

Met midsummer, midway to her second
life may make or break her — tall, equine-
boned, looked much like Maud Gonne to mad me.
Celt to the crown of her held high redhaired
head she fully stopped and turned around
my day and way deliberately . . .
Two clean sheets in a sailing wind . . .
How all wayward wanting will find each
other where and whenever ways cross, yet
must move on. Mating makes for migration . . .
And news from you at last from Old Jamaica
on your way back down under to my ancestral out-
back luxury linered in high hope, deep down doubt
amidships of our midlife's serious sail out.
Who's your pilot now? Now you've cast off all
your landlines, sail down under to slip and start
again? I see you redhead proud on the sundeck
moulding your mystique of the tall, single madonna
in removed silence — scream held within, unheard
by those blue-rinse others going nowhere. We grope.
And you sailed, grande as a Spanish galleon, into my
life like that, on a taverna quarterdeck, stayed
in port where we poured out our pain till we parted.
Yet, only out of the chagrin of chaos and loss may we
make a world. "To do instead of not doing", old E.P.
And finally: "To be men not destroyers." Destroyers
and destroyed our different selves we don't wish that,
with harsh hindsight, on any soul we love. There's always
surely some magic sacred place midway up our mountain,
midmark on the wave, where and when we know to take all
those unchartered constellations of any singular soul as they
rotate in their own knotted navigation where they shine out
if we may sail home to some heart's harbour.

Places

Limerick City

for Jack Donovan

Christmas blazed a bundle of bonfires.
Carousers jumped off bridges for bets
and the City of the Broken Treaty
drifted towards an unknown distinction
up and down the River Shannon.
Along the Flag of All Nations Street
a shadow moved on every threshold
in mysterious inviting relief.
Drawn blinds. No heat from
gaping fireplaces. Flowers
withered in their vases. Occasionally,
in the isolated suffocation
of those blank days,
an incomprehensible vision dawned.
But cautiously, scarcely daring
consideration. Buttoned up,
it brooded about in the rain
pelting up the river.
I believed we were possessed,
unwilling to recognise ourselves
in the dirty mirror
of our own black night —
while all the time,
down on the forbidden docks,
my twentieth century — the real
not our politico-clerical century —
rode at anchor. Prepared to sail.

after Anna Akhmatova

The Old Town

for John Jordan

One night I took a few young fellows,
demons for drink, to a place I frequent
down an alley behind the old-town's warehouses.
It was so late even God had gone to bed
but the landlord woke at my knock. At first
he refused to open. I pleaded with him
by every noble name on the better side
of his family and jingled my money loudly.
That's when he opened up — sure of silver.
Even the door seemed to take pleasure
opening the way he did it and his smile showed
the fang of his greed. "Come in boys",
says he, "and welcome. You're no bother.
The later the safer, as the fellow said."
"The night's gone out of it", I said.
"But home and dry, we'll wet our whistle."
And we settled down until dawn.

after Abu Nuwas

The Wide World

Ignorant of the world
we threw ourselves into it
as a swimmer throws himself
into the sea.

As fishermen do,
we brought with us
bundled belongings
of personal value,
memories mostly.

Ignorant of the world
we fronted it
as a boat the waves,
asked no more
than a chance to live
full lives,
leave some record.

Among the crowded distortions
of indifferent cities we survived
on what we'd brought with us —
provincial sensibility.

Ignorant of the world
we set out across it
as sailors the sea.

Some survived.
Some sank.

Her Daughter at Syracusa

for Giovanna Pellizzi

Here I read *The Greeks and Irrationality*.
Summer begins. Our years have passed —
we've met first time in ten during
this my lonest, darkest ever winter.
Once, since then, we had a day together
through walk-talk. Then you had to leave
for here. On irrational impulse, Irish I
followed and watched you play Euripides.

We talk the Greeks, poetry, your mother —
that clarifies obscurities, perhaps too late.
I tell you anecdotes of Simonides and that
nephew, so despised by Pindar, Baccylides
all here together once and of Sappho's
exile here too like mine and said to you:
     "When I look
       straight at you
       I think even she
       was not so lovely,
       that you are more fine
       but not more fine souled."

Odd as Archilochus, I live alone on this
his island. far from you and your mother
now. What will happen? A Roman woman
playing *The Trojan Women* in Syracusa's
Greek theatre. Your grace confused me
as I fixed-faced across the choric sea
to where I had to go, what I had to do.

We're of an age, love. What will happen?

Café Floccas

She stepped in,
dark skinned, alone.
Myself and my foreign
friend sat talking.
He told us our
names. She's Dora.
Says she's leaving
a while this evening —
some days'
holidays.
I'm leaving today
too, the other way.
Her slow eye
told me
that she
wants company.
Talk over,
we leave together.
I take her
by taxi
to her noisy
street corner.
She's one bag
and an overcoat
for the night boat.
I'd have gone along
but feared no return.
I drive to my own
boat farther on,
take her image
for my voyage —
one ikon
before the tabernacle
of the heart's broken
chapel.

Notes from Naoussa

Evening's now grown dark,
night climbs up our sky
and through my flung wide windows,
in this our room of rooms round here,
the evening sea air's fresco after a scorcher day.
Out in the bay that Saab stutter of fishermen
headed out puts your heart, far off now, back
into my silence. Our whitewashed mud
village houses make squares, cubes, rectangles —
playblocks for mythological giants.

No stars tonight though the sunset looked
like you must have, rooting for chiffon
in your trunkfull before that fancydress
we both were at before I knew you and never
met there, although I, tipsy, noisily
fell head first into the orchestra. You remembered
the confusion years later but were much too busy
that night to bother ask what happened who, off
beyond the carousing throng in some corner
surrounded by attentive admirers as always.

Your long awaited letter arrived today.
I've carried it about till now, unopened.
They've shut our summer season here
and I'm about to open my winter's watch.
Daily now the trains of stumpy donkeys,
like black worrybeads, clatter clearly
through our village with goatskin sacks
of crushed grape juice for the wine-
making. Round our white harbour walls
the men mend nets nonstop — yellow,
saffron, blue — now we've got fine
fishing weather; although Sarandos
bumped his boat badly on rocks last time
homing — wife and child abroad at night —
from six weeks' tuna fishing round Danoussa.
Ripped a bow break flooded his engine,
the strongest in our harbour, only made it
port-safe driving her fully throttle, half under
half out of water, straight up on the night strand . . .

Fallen vine leaves scrape their sound on
my terrace flagstones nights now like the leaves
of your letters scrape about in my soul . . .
Burnt out summer. Oppulent autumn.
As I slit your envelope with my knife
one black moth, then a white one, bumble
in through my open window, find my naked
light bulb, beat about it blindly . . . Familiarity
of your hand's script. I try imagine see you
write it where you live now; you who live
on a typewriter. Sealing and opening
matter most. The content's always known.
Your script scrawls stronger now —
from absence, lone endeavour. Stronger
too your language, argument, your plea
for all that broke between us. All this our
room draws down on me: the small ikon over
our peasant marriage bed, that banded
sea-chest fills the corner, print of a boat
sails into its promising sunset. My work
tables shapes a coffin. This page upon it . . .
Shadows shift closer round our cottage.
That boatman's Saab engine's stopped. Your
gargoyle lines of letter leap out to rail.
I look out over the bible flood of bay
to where that sun sets nightly on our wreck.

I fold these pages. Rise. Put out my lamp.
Lie down under our seaweed bamboo ceiling.
The thought moths burned about the bulb have stopped
their Dionysian dance. Stretched, I stare my inside
silence up into my clay black dark.

Santa Maria Revisited

for Oceanis and Mimis

The house the same — terrace,
strand, sea. Beyond,
our Cycladic archipelago.
our hosts, old friends. Nothing's
changed. Their dog's bark the same,
timeless wash of the waves, this
house's full hospitality, creak
of the well's wind handle draws
water, our hostess's smile, our host's
huge helpfulness. Nothing's changed
except the lack of noise. No rattle
of a wild small boy rampant about
his curiosities making much mischief.
One small boy shoving the sea away
from the land to let his sky in;
a boy who can't discover, try out
all fast enough before collapsed
exhaustion into sleep. The wind
in the bushes there; wind that rattles
the doors, shifts the sand on the shore;
the cicada at the hour we light the lamps
and the huddle of the houses across the sound
lit by the setting sun. All there.
A stage, curtain up, without its actor:
one small boy dislodging time and space,
human affections and their grace
with busy innocence, noble nonsense.

The Mountain

Late afternoon. Sun spangles the sea.
Sick with the black circle of habit, I
make for the mountain. Thoughts
awkward as rocks in this unmanageable head.

First, marked stone tracks
through scrub and slate-flakes,
past the last hill holdings; then —
trust in the sign of surefootedness —
black goat dung for direction
and follow the sun round the sheltered
shoulder not to be caught by darkness.

High up, meeting the goat herd's
descent for the evening's milking.
Sweet cacophony of goat bells. The herdsman
calling out to the strays — his cry
carries for miles over the stillness.
Baggy trousered, broad brimmed
hat shape of a medieval helmet,
his raised arms hang by his wrists
on his stick stretched straight
across his shoulders — his face
the make, the colour of mountains.

Goat bells in half light.
Each lithe goat with his own
bell note fits his hoofs' dance.
Strong scent of the thyme shrub.
Sometimes a goat skull, or a dog skull.

Steep last slope.
Sight of the summit.
Arrival. Panorama.
Wind from the open sea. Strong
sense of accomplishment . . .
Rough inscriptions found cut
crudely on flat stones;
an attempt to read some significance . . .

Sunset. Moonrise.
Eat and roll out
covers to sleep in.
Presence of time in the silence —
of man's mortality, of the mountain's god.
Dark anchorite of the soul.

Stretched on the mountain,
face to the stars, I am
in the middle of my life . . .

Music below in the bay.
Skip and step of country boys
at the goat dance.
As lights go out, you,
this night below in the village,
turn to our bed alone . . .

Somewhere, a donkey, blindfolded,
treads his endless circle
tackled to his waterwheel . . .

The void, terror, at the lack of you.
There's a barbarism in love
lovers inflict on each other.
No agrandisement of personal vanity
merits the agony of that human hardship.

To live full lives,
taking nothing to excess;
to face beauty and barbarism
maintaining in the mind
whatever may save from
the emergence of imminent evil;
to balance between society's shocks
and the spirit's serenity;
live by heart and head and hand —
resolution in this . . .

Sleep . . .

Wake to sunrise, moonset;
sweet cacophony of the goatbells' return,
the herdsman's call to the strays —
cut of him traversing the mountainside
bulky as boulders.

Urgently roll up the covers.
Urgent descent in early sunlight.
Urgency! Urgency!
Then the naked plunge
into the sea
like a biblical baptism.

My Country

Although they have smashed our sacred statues,
have burned us out from our hold places
our gods are not therefore dead.
They still guide us.
Their very souls still remember.
Their strength soaks our air.

Sure as day dawns
shadows of heroic youth,
faint at first,
but with surer step,
generation after generation
stride across every field.

after C. P. Cavafy

Sahara

for Doris Shoukri

Sand. Sand grained as seasalt, tawny as lionskins,
wild all that way to my horizon lashes' line.
In the swept sky's eye its whitegold pupil centres.

Here's no sand our childhood beaches might define
where all our aweful ocean couched down quiet
sometimes, nor unmapped desert, children will imagine,

drowned in dream, each dreamed Arabian Night,
but all that ageless roll of hilldune, plain,
wadi crusted under this straight sun's killer light.

Desert shale and sand's my span open
sea's antithesis — tireless, endless, empty save
for me and sometimes, far off, some lone

other, proud on horseback or kinship camel drove,
clear in clean Church colours — white
and black, scarlet, purple — live

in the day's relentless length and light
like one lone fisherman in his tar black
currach or some brightly painted fleet

of strung out fishing smack
come from where, you'd ask,
or headed for? Horsemen and caravan tack

their talk and desert's rise, fall and risk
as boatmen do and cross their sea. Antithesis
too in that they both boast movement, mood and mask.

The desert's constant shifts in sounds of silence,
the sea's in silent sound, when we're out in them.
Bright day unmasks night's shunt and shove of difference.

But though their each security, serenity's the same
for every restless spirit, we, in our common frame
of nature, dread them poked ferocious, plunged insane.

People

Headmistress

The wind, risen,
drives in southwest,
I start early through our woken
village round the bay with bookbag, crust-
bag, hardboiled eggs and bottles for lunch.

Children, all starch,
kimono, lunchbox,
battle through the drystone arch,
flagstone street up hill to their schoolhouse.
I carry my schoolhouse in my lost son's bookbag.

I look far back
for years to when
I'd head for fiercefaced Mrs. Veriker
and St. Michael's School beyond the Corn-
Market. One fellow from then I remember,

now *sparks* on a tanker.
Another, a girl.
met by chance — I failed to know her —
my last time there, at a country session festival.
Her redhaired brother we, tough boys, nicknamed *Rashers*.

We played Saturdays
at Tarzan and Jane
in Feathereye's Store. One winter's day
I met Penny Bun passing Chapel Lane.
She said: "there's no school. It burned down

last night." The dream
of every schoolboy.
It had. And upright in a stream
of firemen's water, too tender tough to cry,
Mrs. Veriker pronounced "Evacuation!"

Memories' migration . . .
In those War days
at night on the wireless I thought the static
real men fighting. Our shelf's three books: *The Lays*

*and Legends of Thomond, The Arabian Nights, The Seven
Pillars of Wisdom . . .*
No one's around.
Lunch done, walk on.
Afternoon. Back in our village I'll find
the children of memory bundling
out of the schoolhouse for home.

Son

I have watched you,
brazen as brass,
blond as sovereigns,
upstart of beauty
who once, gallavanter,
galloped bareback the sows
squealing wild from the sty —
eager grip on their earlugs.
Watched you proud as a pup
when evening light folds
westward, when redhead
hyacinth quilt down our
hills from their distances,
like old family dogs to our
lazy evening hearthstones.

Cratlow Wood at growth and crackle,
placid Plassy Bank sees us together
cross Thomond Bridge — the towers
of King John's Castle at your
small boy's back as I tell you
the story of Drunken Thady and
the Bishop's Lady reciting Hogan.
All testimony to our horrid history.
St. Munchin's, the Broken Treaty Stone
tell of our beginnings, treachery, end,
right before you. On the shoulder
Of Shannon's walls the older gulls
stand upright on one wrinkle-bandy leg
while the younger wheel and dive,
grey in the sun's last declining.
The trees splay bare. Fallen
leaves compost in piles.

The Norman square
on square of St. Mary's
bell tower shoulders
our westerly sky.

My son, stride on
where once
I strode
likewise.

Fathers and Sons

for Leonard

Driven here
by the west wind —
landbirds from starboard
crossed our bow. In the hope
of friendly days to come,
we've settled.

Our place fronts the shore in this
our sea dingle. The north wind
curls whitecaps length of the breakwater.
Bed, table, chair and the journey's
history. I keep big blackbacked
notebooks, look like chiselled
flagstones, for logbooks.

Comes a day in age's privilege
when father and son may talk —
after the trial of absence,
the pain suffered for lack.

Void of all baseness yourself,
you watched over me a child.
Now, for all my quarrelman manner,
I watch over you,
your hangdog age.

In your years' cloud of pain
that grey head's filled with countless
preoccupations. The smallest chore
becomes some laboured project.

We talk:
You of our native fields, the simple
daily events of our people; I
of my world travelled and laboured.

Your grandson beside us grows daily.
My woman's more beautiful yearly.
After much knocking about
where's she'll mend me?

His plan's plot decided: straight spoked as thistle spikes.
Aggressive his intention, touchy as a hedgehog,
he nailed on the table his head's set notion
for crosstalk, then broke the breadth of that Ocean
begins beyond our western bog.

There he dug his dollar then got back. His likes
not known down our way. Firbolg blocky,
he roofed and rigged a Famine razed ruin
to house his haltered woman. Bulky
as treetrunks, he bested stone and rain,

his leery locals, to force his fistsize farm work.
By day he ploughs unbroken ground;
at night his hammered headstrong home.
He knows the pack's stacked score cards down:
the harness that's his heartscald land;

survival's perennially saved and sheltered harvest; the muck
through manic winter after; spring's soft seedtime
and lovers' hopes for love's short halter;
summer's wait-out watch God's rigged game.
That's his here-and-now and hereafter.

His Wife

Blackhaired. Her broad eyes flash clear faience.
High-cheeked her eyes' bone. A splash rain shower
her laughter. She's his true good wife. Softer
than old men's palaver plays her smile's glance

disarmed of any sort of weaponry. Matchless
her glad grace, open as wounds her gift heart
in home hurt, friends' grief, joy's loss. No insert
her talk's tame words of the casual thoughtless.

Her concern's Christian for all beggared kind
and her farm hearth's open. Landmade men
her background, husband, children. No craven
city doubt warps her vowed once only love bond.

We men odd times each orbit prodigal.
She guards the haggard, upholds the house wall.

Commander Oscar Bacichi

Old seawolf, grande as a galleon,
his general compass cut as a sextant's
collage of man's Oceans. The cartography
of his face, marked as a navigator's map, held
together like the weather-beaten planks of a ship's hold.
His nose a noble navalman's cartouche; his foghorn voice
the drop of anchors. Seafaring reader, his refined
hands spread broad as open books. By bunk
and bed Montaigne his Bible. His land manners
the history of the Austro-Hungarian Empire:
all class, little cash, honourable credit.
He brandished a monocle, easy as an eyeglass,
in his one droop eye on a black silk ribbon,
ensconced at the café would drop it dramatically
into his newspapers for the cruise past of each
cruiser beauty full sail through Sunday morning's sunlight.
Till the day he died — one year older than God, he claimed —
he lived with his obdurate virgin sister —
all roar, no rancour — stamped his obverse.
Present as his landlocked ship's figurehead,
she always gruffed us buck cabinboys welcome aboard.
And he'd surely have foundered some night but for her.
In his room, rigged his cabin, he'd chart the day's course
every morning. On the town's open sea philistines sailed
close risked his broadside. Having none of his own,
children followed his tack wake like seagulls a liner.
Redhaired young ladies with freckles could easily
scuttle his huge heart's timbers whenever they cut
cross his bowsprit and did. His logbook ends
with one entry: "I dock and hand over."

Robert Lowell in Rome

After your reading — the Alexander fourteeners
so apropos in Rome, we repaired for glasses of Roman
wine Portico d'Ottavia the Jewish ghetto. Lady Caroline
trailed along like a pregnant Irish setter holding your hand.
You seemed happy as a lunatic with his nurse in our daily
madhouse. We talked of what we were plotting at. "Long lines",
you said, "day by day". That night to dinner outdoors in soft
Santa Maria Trastevere with Rafael Alberti and our three
muses. Our talk of Franco's Spain, Vietnam, Neruda,
E.P. silent in Venice. You'd known Alberti in Brazil long before.
Then after some drinks back at his house the muddled
meander round to your Hotel Medusa. That's the last time
we met and talked. Now I talk to you this way.

A. Roland Holst

Eighty oddish, he lives
alone in the country
not far from the sea:
two rooms, kitchen, bathroom,
his books, his music.

He received us dressed
like an Irish country gentleman
and joked about friends.
With the help of a few Genevers
I told him his old pal Frummel
called him a Cardinal in the Church
of W. B. Yeats. He replied: "Then Wolfgang's
a high priest in the Church
of Stefan Georg. But of all
Prime Ministers, Goethe
ranks the best poet."

Over his door the straw cross
of the Irish St. Brigid. We talk . . .
Later, out to dinner,
we talk poets and poetry.
He says: "I prefer Dylan Thomas
to T. S. Eliot, especially poems
like *Lament*. You know,
when I was young and green
the erotic and the spiritual
walked hand in hand for me
and found harmony. With age,
the erotic faded and I feared
the spiritual would desert me too.
I was wrong. The spiritual
filled the vacuum and I've found
serenity in my last days."
He paused. "But I don't ride my beloved
Dutch bicycle anymore for fear of falling off."

After dinner, mellowed with good
gin, good wine and kitchen, we part.
He returns to two rooms, books, music,
bed, table, straw cross
and his achieved serenity.

He's done it. Did it waving
gently down his final long-drop
though he swore he wouldn't, that noon
over wine, Spoleto, Italy, crackling whiskey
still from mad Ireland and the Dublin pubs his
hero Yeats never entered, knew, wrote of
or could, unlike Joyce. And I believed him.
Sort of. How disbelieve such brave, brazen
beard-head, beatified hands of a maker,
crowfoot eyes like Irish seaboard inlets
of my childhood? Because of the children,
he said and told me his father's suicide
story from his childhood. And I believed him.

Forty below and the Mississippi frozen,
his specs folded into his pocket and one
work walking black passerby on the early
morning bridge to wave his forever farewells to.

Umm Kalthoum

I sat at an old coffee table
down Cairo's City of the Dead.
My coffee black as charcoal
thick as bogmen. The landlord

waiter, Nubian, played his old
scrape pickup. Umm Kalthoum
sang out. Haunt of the held
drone, long length high, then down

her scale. That steady voice
dark as mosques, deep
as messianic mystery. Each poise
note held, then drop —

as the bowstring drops down
the instrument plays it.
Voice of love, her religion,
her people. Her way of it

miracles millions. From home
her father's passed down tradition.
She sang out The Book. The same
sound style seannós came down

to my time, Ireland. Memories
of old men, quiet women, in country
kitchens intoned long night hours.
Bend of that ancient language beyond me.

I copy them still at times
humming alone in foreign places.
Her language beyond me, Kalthoum's sound seems
natural soil of my native memories.

Lovers at night desert their beds
in the dark, slip silently out from
shut rooms, listen to the words
of Umm Kalthoum. I'm now among them.

George Anthony Palmer 1901-1976

Your last book arrived today: the posthumous
collection of your own choice put together finally
by friends you taught sincerity, devotion, high regard,
and how to read. I deep lament your passing,
George, I'd hoped to see you once again there,
where we'd work at words mornings, but preferably
here where all the beautiful things of Europe delight:
Our walks and talks in Rome. Reading in Venice
with Ezra after dinner and boating about the canals.
You gave me the deeply needed refuge of your
hospitable mind and home in America where I felt
so insecure and told me how you went to the trenches
of the Great War at fifteen, faking your age. I remember
a photo of you in uniform. Handsome idealist. Romantic
adventurer. That never changed. The adventure changed
to all that's beautiful in our warring world you've left.
Poetry is difficult. No one knew that better, harder.
Like Yeats, you died revising. Unlike Pound and Graves.
You believing, talking, still trying. That's example, as you
were example in all things elegant. Even in death.
I'd wanted much to see you one last time to play
a tune but I'll see you one day on Fiddler's Green.

Pablo Neruda Arrives

Await his arrival, then take him straight
to Rafael Alberti's — every Spaniard's home
from home. Yevtushenko waits too — tall, all
Euclidic angles, schoolboy mischief grin. Stalked
around Florence his closing circle until beside her
heel to heel he: "You grow jealous, no?" to me.
"Zenia, I'll dance your Russian rhymed line Irish
round any muse we choose any day, night or place
we together toss up win or lose." Bullfighter
without a bull. The beautiful women of poets. Then
Neruda and wife Matilda benignly through bureaucracy's
barriers — he rotund Cordio de Los Andes, she
opulent South American beauty and passion,
serenity's smile of the Muse master mistress.
"I adore the dull English with their pubs closed
at five for afternoon" Pablo. But not
the English left millions you've seen rot in Indian mud.
Then Zenia again, all raw royal Russian provincial
gentleman of the world. There's brazen bedamned
understanding in the bedlam bedouin of poets' give
and take equal till death do us part. And it doesn't,
friend. It does not do us part. Farewell.

Missing Andrei Voznesensky at Rome Festival '79

We met in Italy's Firenze in that grand
Camera del Cinquecento, Pallazzo della Signoria,
at another Festival. Tonight I miss you, not here
with our mutual friend Yevtushenko, looks plumper.
We, the youngest then in Firenze among those grey-
haired old dogs of the battle from East and West —
stubborn, strongheaded. I knew of your Moscow crowd
thumbing noses at bullyboy bosses, Khruschev and Surkov,
singing out in Mayakovsky Square to your generation
a chorus-glad praise for him and Isaak Babel, Mandelshtam,
friends Akhmatova, Pasternak . . . So many!

Cosmopolitan provincials both, from far flung off places,
in Florence's Renaissance centre among our peers
and elders, I stood minded of the day, as important
to me, I met my first poet: Patrick Kavanagh playing
rings and darts in his Dublin pub among honest friends.
(Later I helped him out a door Tvardovski tried to get
in through.) And that evening, together, we recited in turn.
You, stocky spreadlegged, white hands on hips, head
thrown back, like a Cycladic figurine playing flute,
in defiance. Giving it out for your time, face
to face with that grey-haired scowl of Caesar
Censor Surkov — blood on his dirty hands.
"Ya Goya" "I am Goya / of the bare field /
gouged by the enemy's beak." No merchant
of protest jargon you, but of human rights,
love, death, the trespass of the State, blind
authority, cheap despair: "banging your body /
like a tolling bell / against the toll of insults. /
It hurts but it resounds." Immediately Surkov's up
reciting his stale Stalinish verses, his pigbuyer's
chapped face all grin like a death's head false Yorick,
at gravestone blank faces of his European and Party peers.
And Murillo Mendes jumped up to recite in angry answer
of common Christian love, dignity, freedom of the human spirit.

The night would have exploded into East-West war had not
handsome, legendary Nazim Hikmet swung to the rescue
a smiling Hittite — rest in peace — singing his ironies in that
Turkish nobody understood at all but rose in response to and brought
us all back to our common reality:
makers of poetry, not buyers of war.

Paraphernalia

Holiday Resort

These were baths. Today,
not even the wind's pampered here
and these whitewashed stains
barely remember the tennis shorts
and the traps of women's revealed underwear.

To us who know,
these aren't even malignant spirits
because, for some time now,
they've found sustenance here
in humidity and mould,
where ceiling and floor
look the same.

In the courtyard the collapsed walls
reveal a hunchback wearing a dead man's suit.
He's chopped down all the trees,
cleared the shrubbery so they won't force him
to sweep up the leaves in autumn.

after Vladmir Holan

Day Trip

for Robert Cabot

Short sleep. Wake
while the rest sleep.

Push out the boat
south for the island.
Landfall. Beach her.
The goatherd strides to greet us
his welcome over sea shingle —
his smile of shone obsidion.

We all join the women
shelter side of their stone
hut houses, lick vanilla in
glasses of fresh well water.
We present our mainland gifts:
American cigarettes for the men
chocolate and sweet shop cake
for the women and tell them the news.
They're the only family on this
island and their thousand goats.

The women wear black. White
headscarfs half cover their faces.
The one child — forty years
an idiot daughter — squats alone,
grins against the far wall.
She won't budge. They're five
people forty odd years on this
bare rock alone . . .
But they've made a hearth that's
hospitality lost to our world.

Agave

for Patrick Gallagher

By the seashore
that seacrow
caws on the topmost
flower of the agave;
throws her shadow
across my path.

In Greece
of blood in broad daylight,
the agave is the flower
rises from the maw
of the Medusa cactus;
towers straight up
spring to autumn, then
topples over, dead;
spills its cactus seed
for the next Medusa head.

In Ireland
of blood and battle,
the seacrow is the black
Badhbh goddess destroys;
wings in from over the sea,
circles the marked man battles
his waves, settles
on his beaten bowed head.

That's the sign
he's finally dead.

The Ruin

The sun scorches today outside.
I sit indoors with pen and paper. You,
however, though far from me now, still
bask in my desperate imagination —
proud, pigtailed like an Indian squaw.

Autumn and the fallen vineleaves, crisp
brown on the white stone, rustle
memories of us here together yearly.

Ours was a time few have relished;
a rich time of penniless passion:
sea crossing and land crossing
and the warmth of genuine welcome;
the basis of history to build on
and the glory that's children growing.
Now we have only the rubble of personal
history — places void of you or me like
sanctuaries abandoned by their gods.
What's barbarian in our time
galloped its madness over us
and all's destruction, scattered.

For so much sunshine here
this place is gloom and guideless.
Nothing grows or echoes and the wind
laments as through old ruins.
Ruined, I stop this construct here
and leave what's left
unfinished . . .

Inheritance

We grew up familiar with our past's shadows,
familiar with our people's tradition for secrets —
learned to read their significance,
to nourish them like desire and longing
in a backward place with no future.

Wide-eyed in bed in the darkness,
under the unquenchable flame of the votive
lamps, we stared at the olive eyes
of the holy pictures that smoulder
all night in their corners.
And we believed them.

We were given two images to worship:
the spouse of sorrow and the golden girl
in visionary songs of the past.
And we believed them.

We were told nothing of what
such images may become.

We grew up with native
secrets, unaware of the nightmare.
We learned, in our time, to live
each with his personal nightmare.

Origins

We walked out of ceaseless rain, out of
grey featureless towns into the long
light of the northern summer and found
the fields in the fullness of their season.
We were never the same again.

We surveyed panoramas of low stone walls
numerous and varied as old men's wrinkles;
watched pigeons in piebald flocks
flap about farmyards as children
round church doors on Sundays;
trees looked familiar as locals
and country lanes held a nostalgic
urgency like desire.
When shall we see the same way again?

At one point I realised the sea
lay somewhere beyond all this — a mythology
of stones shored on its beaches;
realised we would some day each
have to pick up the sea shaped
stones one by one for personal
scrutiny: like an archaeologist reading
fragments on an ancient site
or like a stranded sailor
hoping for a washed up bottle
with some sort of message in it.

Farewell

Will my funeral leave from here under
my broken mountain? Who'll pay our
village carpenter to make my coffin and how
will they get it down to the road, now
they've put barbed wire up to keep
the donkeys in and out? They'll have
to hire one of our friends' caïques
to carry me across the bay to the village.
The people will gather to gape in the square,
especially the school kids I keep the foreign stamps
for. Our harbour will be full of sun and
bright fishing boats and the café full
with the Captains and their tall tales as I'm
carried round the village for my last look,
the coffin open — our custom here — and farewell.
Then it's up our Stony Batter to The Stony Joke.

I have been happy in this hospitable harbour,
this scrummaged village below my broken mountain.
Friends of our homely café drink deep for me this night.
I wish you all long life.

after Nazim Hikmet